IDENTIFYING

ANGLERS' FLIES

The new compact study guide and identifier

IDENTIFYING

ANGLERS' FLIES

The new compact study guide and identifier

Stephen J. Simpson and George C. McGavin

Edited by Peter Gathercole

CHARTWELL
BOOKS, INC.

A QUINTET BOOK

Published by Chartwell Books
A Division of Book Sales, Inc.
114, Northfield Avenue
Edison, New Jersey 08837

This edition produced for sale
in the U.S.A., its territories
and dependencies only.

ISBN 0-7858-0772-1
Reprinted 1998
This book was designed and produced by
Quintet Publishing Limited
6 Blundell Street
London N7 9BH

Creative Director: Richard Dewing
Designer: James Lawrence
Editor: Peter Gathercole
Project Editor: Diana Steedman
Photographers: Keith Waterton and Peter Gathercole

The material in this book previously appeared in
The Angler's Fly Identifier by Stephen J. Simpson and
George C. McGavin

Typeset in Great Britain by
Central Southern Typesetters, Eastbourne
Manufactured in Singapore by
Bright Arts (Singapore) Pte Ltd
Printed in China by
Leefung-Asco Printers Ltd

CONTENTS

INTRODUCTION

Of all the problems which confront the fly fisher perhaps the most confusing is fly choice. It is the great variable, made no easier by the simply vast number of patterns available. You may well have a perfect grasp of the correct tackle to use, which fly line, reel and rod but the decision as to which pattern of fly is going to be the most effective is one which must be made every time a line is cast.

However, there are logical steps which may be taken to make this choice simpler and more straightforward. The first is to identify just what the fish are feeding on. This guide is designed to eliminate much of the hit and miss of fly choice and is achieved by first listing the major groups of insects, other invertebrates, and small fish which make up the trout's diet and by including relevant and effective imitations.

Trout are essentially opportunist feeders preying upon those creatures which are the most numerous or easily consumed. All kinds of aquatic insects, crustaceans and fish are taken along with land borne creatures such as spiders, beetles, caterpillars – indeed anything small and vulnerable which falls or is blown on to the water's surface.

RIGHT: Fly fishing is a sport of observation and interpretation. Which pattern to use is a decision to make each time a line is cast.

WHY FLY CHOICE IS IMPORTANT

There are times when the trout's feeding pattern can become very specific. If a particular creature proliferates, as happens during a hatch of mayflies or caddisflies, trout can become preoccupied with that particular item. This in turn means that to fool the trout you must fish a good imitation of that insect and fish it in a natural way.

This link between insect hatches and the artificial fly is intrinsic to fly fishing. To take full advantage of the situation, it is important for the fly fisher to have a basic knowledge of entomology. There is no need, however, to be able to identify every species of insect out in the field. Indeed attempting to do so can be totally counterproductive and in many cases is almost impossible. What is important is to have an understanding of what the different groups look like, their shape, size, and color variations.

Although many types of insects and other invertebrates are all potential food items for the trout, the most important may be divided into six major groups. These, in order of general importance, are the mayflies, Order Ephemeroptera;

the true flies, Order Diptera; the caddis or sedge flies, Order Tricoptera; the stoneflies, Order Plecoptera; the dragonflies and damselflies, Order Odonata; and the freshwater shrimps or scuds, Order Crustacea. Other food types, such as Corixae, beetles, grasshoppers, snails, small fish, alderflies, leeches, ants, and moths can be very important at specific times, but overall do not perform such an important role as components of their diet.

This book is divided into two sections. The first deals with those fly patterns designed to imitate specific food forms. Throughout the world of trout fishing there are a variety of creatures, mostly invertebrates, which are regularly taken by trout, and while the actual species vary from country to country their form, color, and habits do not.

The second section deals with more general patterns; flies which will catch trout in a variety of conditions and water types. When there is no obvious hatch or no other clue as to what the trout are taking this group of patterns provides a solid base from which to start.

THE MAIN FOOD GROUPS

ABOVE: A mayfly sub-imago.

THE MAYFLIES

The Mayflies: Order Ephemeroptera, range in size from ⅛ to 1½ inches long. The adults have delicate cylindrical bodies with either two or three tails. The legs are long and slender and the wings, of which there are two pairs in most species, the front pair being large and triangular, are held vertically at rest. This resting posture has led to the mayflies' alternative common name of up-wings.

As far as the angler is concerned, mayflies have three main stages in their lives, the nymph, the sub-imago and the imago. The nymph is aquatic and usually brown or olive in coloration to blend in with its environment. The sub-imago can be anything from white to bright yellow though by far the most common is various shades of olive. Sub-imago is a transitionary stage between nymph and true adult and is the stage referred to in a hatch. The imago is the sexually mature stage, normally more brightly colored than the sub-imago.

The many species (worldwide 2,500) inhabit varied water types, depending on the species, from small ponds to rich chalk streams and fast flowing rocky rivers. In fact many of the nymphs have evolved to live in very specific habitats, some being flattened to allow them to cling to rocks in fast currents. Some species are able to burrow in sand or silt, while others are more active, able to dart about through weed beds.

The fact that the mayflies are widely distributed, many species occurring in the same water types populated by trout, and that populations may be vast makes them the most important group for fly fishers to identify and to imitate.

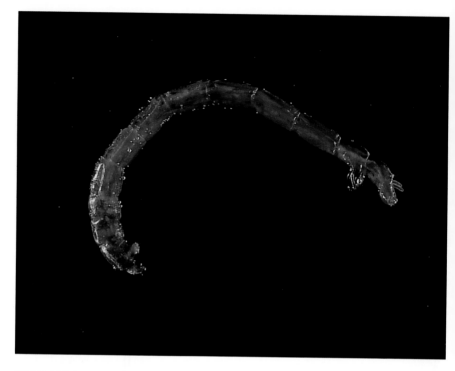

THE TRUE FLIES

The true flies (Diptera) are a vast Order encompassing a wide range of aquatic and terrestrial species. Of the aquatic types the non-biting or Chironomid midge is the most important to the angler. Especially on lakes and reservoirs the various species of Chironomid are found throughout the year in vast numbers and make up a large part of the trout's diet.

The three main stages are the larvae, a small worm-like creature up to ½ inch long and either green, brown, or bright red in color, the pupa and the winged adult. Although all three stages are taken by the trout it is the larva and the pupa which are the most widely imitated.

Other species, which are semi-aquatic or terrestrial, include the crane fly or daddy-longlegs, plus fully terrestrial insects such as the bluebottle and drone fly and bibionids including the hawthorn fly, and black gnat.

ABOVE: Bloodworms, Chironomid midge larvae, are named from their red respiratory pigment.

CADDISFLIES

Caddis or sedge flies, Order Tricoptera, are drably colored moth-like insects, which, like moths, are most often seen as adults toward dusk and into dark. They are to be found on all water types inhabited by trout and therefore make up a significant part of their diet.

Adult caddisflies vary in color from black, to almost white though various shades of brown are, by far, the most common. Size varies from micro-caddis at only ⅛ inch through to 1½ inches long with the wings held low over the body in tent-like fashion when at rest.

The three stages of interest to the angler are the aquatic larva and pupa plus the winged adult. The larvae vary greatly in size and color and while some are free-swimming, many build cases from sand, small stones or pieces of plant material to protect their delicate bodies. The pupae are able swimmers and are normally, amber, green, or a dirty-white in color.

ABOVE: The caddis larva will build its protective
case from aquatic plant material.

STONEFLIES

Stoneflies, Order Plecoptera, are basically a drab, brown, or gray in color though a few species are much brighter being quite golden or even bright yellow. They vary in size from only ¼ inch up to 2 inches in length.

There are only two stages which interest the angler, the nymph and the adult. The nymph, often called the creeper, is the aquatic stage, and although not an active swimmer is found clinging to rocks where it feeds, depending on the species, on algae, decaying plant material or small invertebrates.

The nymph has the two tails and cylindrical, slightly flattened body of the adult, only the wings are missing which can be seen enclosed within noticeable wing cases in the fully developed stage.

The adults are not strong fliers preferring to crawl around bankside rocks and vegetation, and at rest the wings are held flat over the back of the abdomen.

In the cool, well-oxygenated rivers and streams which stoneflies favor both the nymphs and adults form a very important part of the trout's diet, especially during late spring and early summer.

ABOVE: Stonefly nymphs do not swim, a fact to keep in mind when fishing their imitations.

DAMSELFLIES AND DRAGONFLIES

Damselflies and Dragonflies, Order Odonata, are highly predatory insects found on both rivers and lakes, though it is the latter where they form the highest proportion of the trout's diet.

The highly camouflaged nymphs inhabit weed beds or bottom silt where they lie in wait for small invertebrates which they grab with a wicked pair of hinged pincers known as the labium.

Although closely related, the damselfly nymphs can be differentiated from those of the dragonfly by having a much slimmer abdomen tipped with three leaf-shaped gills. As adults they can be told apart by the fact that the damselfly holds its four, even-length wings over its abdomen, when at rest, while those of the dragonfly are held sideways, away from the body.

ABOVE: Despite the beauty of adult damselflies, it is the nymphs that are of prime interest to the angler.

CRUSTACEANS

Shrimps, waterlice and crayfish, Order Crustacea. These freshwater aquatic forms of a vast and varied group of invertebrates make up a large proportion of the trout's diet. Shrimps, or scuds as they are also known, are small curved-bodied creatures, flattened from side to side, which inhabit clear rivers and lakes. Shrimps are generally shades of translucent brown or gray and range in size from ¼ to ¾ inch in length.

Waterlice, often called hoglice, are not such capable swimmers as shrimps and prefer a slower weedier environment and are generally found in lakes and slower moving rivers.

Crayfish, which are more predatory and resemble a miniature lobster have a tough protective shell and a strong pair of pincers. Even these though are not enough to ward off an attack from a large trout.

ABOVE: Freshwater shrimp, or scud. The artificial imitation should be fished around weed beds.

FLY FISHING TECHNIQUES

ABOVE: Looking for likely spots on a rocky upland stream.

Just as there are various types of fly there are various techniques for fishing them. Much depends on the water being fished and the behavior of the trout at the time. The ultimate aim is to present a fly in a most natural manner at the same level as that in which the trout are feeding.

Fly fishing techniques may be broken down into two major groups: those used on rivers and those used on still waters such as lakes and reservoirs.

When presenting a fly on a river the greatest problem comes from the flow rate of the water. For river trout fishing a floating fly line is the most commonly used. The fly itself may be fished right on the surface – a dry fly; in the surface – a terrestrial or emerger; or under the surface – a wet fly, nymph or streamer.

When presenting a dry fly or emerger to a fish it must be done drag free. When an insect hatches off or lands on the surface the only forces acting upon it are the current and possibly a breeze and the insect simply follows a path directly downstream. To fool a fish this is exactly how our fly should drift. However, when we cast at a fish another force acts upon our fly – the line.

The line, once it has been cast slightly across the flow, begins to be grabbed by the current. It drags, eventually causing the fly to move faster than the actual current. This acceleration usually results in the fish refusing the fly because it is acting unnaturally. To counteract drag, a snaky line should be cast a few feet upstream of the fish so that there is enough slack to give time for the fly to drift back naturally. This is the principle of upstream dry fly fishing.

A similar method can be used for presenting a nymph. This time the problem is not so much drag as getting the fly to the trout's feeding depth. When trout are not to be seen rising they will often be feeding close to the bottom. For an imitation to be effective it must be fished at the same level as the trout. This is done by casting a weighted pattern a few feet upstream of where the angler judges a fish to be. As the fly free-drifts downstream it will sink until, again, drag eventually pulls the line and causes the fly to rise. The skill is to judge how long the fly needs to sink to the correct depth. Considerations such as water depth and speed of the current need to be taken into account.

Wet flies, streamers, and sometimes nymphs are fished downstream. Because they sink, and are less prone to drag, these types of flies may be cast below the angler, across the flow, and allowed to swing around with the current: a technique known as down-and-across and good for searching a large stretch of water.

On still waters the same types of fly are used, though different rules apply. When fishing from the bank dry flies, wet flies and nymphs are generally fished on a floating line. Although there is no definite current, the prevailing wind will set up a surface drift which can be used to help present the fly, especially those fished subsurface. Most nymph patterns are fished either singly or in teams on a leader as long as 25 feet, the fly line being cast out across the wind. As the fly line will naturally drift around on the breeze the flies are able to sink to the fish's feeding level.

Dry flies and emerger patterns are fished in a similar fashion though usually on a shorter leader as depth is not a problem. These patterns, like those used on rivers, should first be treated with a liquid or paste floatant to prevent them absorbing water and sinking.

LEFT: Wet fly fishing. The skill is to judge how long the fly needs to sink to the correct depth.

As there is no current any movement of the fly needs to be imparted by the angler. In general, dry flies are not moved at all, the line merely being retrieved to take up any slack. However, nymphs, wet flies and lures are all made a great deal more effective by different retrieve rates.

These rates can vary from slow, steady draws of less than 6 inches at a time to a fast, full blooded strip, where 2 feet or more of line is retrieved with every pull of the hand. Nymphs are usually fished the slowest of all, imitating the movement of the real thing.

Wet flies are fished at a medium pace, and from a drifting boat the line is retrieved slightly faster than the boat is drifting toward the team of flies. In this technique, known as loch style, the rod top is raised at the end of every retrieve just before the line is re-cast. This makes the flies rise in the water and the top dropper fly work seductively in the surface. It is a deadly method on many reservoirs and large natural lakes.

It is the streamers or lures which are usually fished the fastest. Those which are intended to imitate small fish fleeing from a marauding trout are retrieved extremely quickly. General lure patterns are also often fished fast in order to induce a following fish into taking.

ABOVE: On still water, wet flies are generally fished on a floating line.

How To Use This Book

The imitative flies in this book are divided into major insect and organism groups: Mayflies, True Flies, Caddisflies, Stoneflies, Damselflies and Dragonflies, Crustaceans and miscellaneous organisms (including bugs, beetles, grasshoppers, alderflies, moths, small fry.) Each group is coded by a color shade on the page edge:

	Mayflies
	True Flies
	Caddisflies
	Stoneflies
	Damselflies and Dragonflies
	Crustaceans
	Miscellaneous
	Non-imitative patterns

Key To Symbols

The differing stages in an insect's life cycle are of interest to the angler. The following at-a-glance symbols denote the life stages and, in addition, whether an insect or organism has an aquatic or terrestrial life cycle:

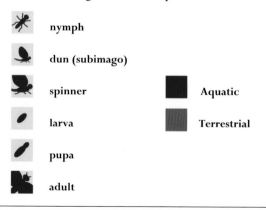

nymph

dun (subimago)

spinner   **Aquatic**

larva   **Terrestrial**

pupa

adult

MAYFLIES

Mayfly Nymph (Walkers)

Dressing

Hook: TMC 5262, size 10-12.
Thread: Brown.
Tail: Pheasant tail fibers.
Body: Cream or off-white wool.
Rib: Brown thread or floss.
Thorax: As body with fibres picked out.
Wingcase: Pheasant tail fibers with ends turned down for legs.

A highly successful pattern representing the nymphs of larger mayfly species with a more cylindrical body form. Move the fly slowly along the bottom, or ascending to the surface to emerge.

Blue-winged Olive Nymph

Dressing

Hook: TMC 100, size 12.
Thread: Gray.
Tail: Blue dun hackle fibers.
Tag: Red wool.
Body: Blue dun wool.
Thorax: Light gray wool.
Wingcase: Pheasant tail fibers.
Hackle: Pale blue dun.

On rivers, fish this pattern on a light floating line casting in the standard down-and-across technique or upstream to fish which can be seen actively feeding on nymphs. If a hatch of adult Blue-winged Olives is in evidence try nymph imitation fished in the surface film.

March Brown Nymph

Dressing

Hook: TMC 100, size 12-14.
Thread: Brown.
Tail: Brown partridge.
Body: Hare's ear.
Rib: Fine gold wire.
Thorax: Hare's ear.
Wingcase: Hen pheasant.
Legs: Hen pheasant fibers tied back.

The nymphs of the March Brown live in fast flowing rocky rivers and for the imitation to be successful it should be allowed to bump along near the bottom. It may be fished on a floating line across the flow suggesting the emerging nymph.

Pheasant Tail Nymph

Dressing

Hook: TMC 100, size 10.
Thread: Brown.
Tail: Pheasant tail fibers.
Body: Pheasant tail fibers.
Rib: Copper wire.
Thorax: Pheasant tail fibers.
Wingcase: Pheasant tail fibers.
Legs: Wingcase dressed over head and tied back to form legs.

This is a classic nymph pattern which can be tied in many sizes. It is best fished very slowly (with a steady figure-of-eight retrieve) to mimic a nymph walking along the bottom. It could also be used as an imitation of a nymph rising to the surface just prior to emergence.

Gold-ribbed Hare's Ear

Dressing

Hook: TMC 100, size 12.
Thread: Brown.
Tail: Hare's mask (long guard hairs).
Body: Dubbed hare's ear.
Rib: Flat fine gold tinsel.

This pattern is incredibly versatile and can be used to suggest either a nymph or emerging dun of a variety of species. Fish it on a floating line either dead drift or with an ultra-slow retrieve. For fishing right in the surface film, the body can be teased out and a floatant applied.

Mayfly Emerger

Dressing

Hook: TMC 5262, size 10-12.
Thread: Brown.
Tail: Three tips of white ostrich.
Body: Cream dubbing blend.
Rib: Brown thread or floss.
Thorax: Cream dubbing blend.
Wings: A few natural or white cul-de-canard feathers tied in by the butts and pulled down.

A marvelous imitation of an emerging mayfly. Fish the pattern so that the body is just below the surface and the wings project above. Imagine that the insect has only just struggled free from its nymphal shuck and is in the process of inflating and expanding its wings. Leave the pattern to drift.

Olive Comparadun

Dressing

Hook: TMC 100, size 14-20.
Thread: Olive.
Tail: Deer hair.
Body: Medium olive dubbing fur.
Thorax: Medium olive dubbing fur.
Wing: Deer hair flared 180° around the top of the hook.

This pattern can be used to mimic a newly emerged dun or one in the process of struggling free of its shuck. Treat with floatant. The wings provide a useful surface indicator. Leave the fly to drift or twitch it to represent the emerging insect's struggles.

Mayfly Dun

Dressing

Hook: TMC 5262, size 10-12.
Thread: Brown.
Tail: Three pheasant tail fibers tied long.
Body: Buff goose feather fibers.
Rib: Brown thread or floss.
Hackles: 1st – dyed green partridge or mallard breast feather; 2nd – natural red game hackle; 3rd – orange short-fibered cock hackle.

A useful imitation of a newly emerged mayfly dun its bright color makes it a great "change" pattern to be used when trout have been refusing more natural colored imitations.

Mayflies

Adams

Dressing

Hook: TMC 100, size 10-20.
Thread: Black.
Tail: Brown and grizzly cock hackle fibers.
Body: Gray fur.
Wing: Two grizzly hackle points tied upright.
Hackle: Brown and grizzly cock hackles.

This superb pattern can be used to represent the dun or spinner of a wide number of mayfly species. The fly should be treated well with floatant and cast a short distance upstream of any rising fish allowing it to drift downstream without any drag. Use a floating line, and as accuracy is the key, a short steeply tapering leader.

CDC Dun

Dressing

Hook: TMC 100, size 14-20.
Thread: Gray.
Body: Gray, cream, or olive wool.
Thorax: Gray, cream, or olive wool.
Wing: Natural gray cul-de-canard.
Hackle: Natural gray cul-de-canard.

The soft downy texture of cul-de-canard feather is ideal for winging dun imitations such as this. It is a simple fly which uses differing size and body color to represent various mayfly species. Fish it singly on a light floating line. The natural oil in the feather will make the addition of any extra floatant unnecessary.

March Brown Dun

Dressing

Hook: 79704 BR, size 12-20.
Thread: Black.
Tail: Partridge hackle fibers.
Body: Hare's ear.
Rib: Gold wire.
Wings: Dark hen pheasant for male and light for female.
Hackle: Dark partridge.

A specific imitation of the march brown dun it is also effective as a general dry fly or when fished during hatches of other small to medium sized mayfly species. As the name suggests the natural hatches during March and early April with midday to early afternoon the peak time to see the duns.

Lunn's Particular

Dressing

Hook: 79764 BR, size 16-20.
Thread: Brown.
Tail: Red game fibers.
Body: Stripped hackle stem.
Wings: Two blue dun hackle tips tied outstretched.
Hackle: Red game cock.

This pattern could represent either a small mayfly dun or spinner. Treat with floatant and fish it so that it sits low in the surface. It can be fished blind over likely looking areas or cast upstream of rising fish and allowed to drift with the current.

Blue-winged Olive Thorax

Dressing

Hook: TMC 100, size 14-20.
Thread: Olive.
Tail: Blue dun hackle fibers tied forked.
Body: Medium olive dubbing blend.
Thorax: Medium olive dubbing blend.
Wing: Natural cul-de-canard or gray turkey flats.
Hackle: Blue dun cock.

Fish either on the surface or in the surface film to mimic anything from a spinner to a stillborn or emerging dun. Fish it during hatches of the natural Blue-winged Olive cast into the path of rising fish.

Mayfly Spinner

Dressing

Hook: TMC 5262, size 10-12.
Thread: Brown.
Tail: Three pheasant tail fibers tied long.
Body: Cream or off-white wool.
Rib: Brown thread or floss.
Hackle: One long-fibered badger cock hackle.

Trout feeding on the natural mayfly spinner can be extremely selective and will only take a fly which is sitting low, right in the surface film. For this reason it can pay to trim off some of the hackle fibers underneath the hook. Prime time for this fly is toward evening. Look for swarms of male spinners dancing around waterside vegetation.

Mayflies

Greenwell's Glory

Dressing

Hook: 79704 BR, size 12.
Thread: Olive or waxed pale primrose thread.
Body: Olive floss or waxed pale primrose thread.
Rib: Fine gold wire or fine gold oval.
Wings: Two pale starling wing slips tied forward and separated.
Hackle: Greenwell's hackle.

This pattern was designed to imitate a number of medium sized mayflies often referred to as olives due to their coloration. It should be treated with floatant and fished singly on a floating line cast into possible holding spots or upstream of a rising fish. Allow to drift with the current.

White-winged Pheasant Tail

Dressing

Hook: TMC 100, size 14-16.
Thread: Brown.
Tail: Tips of the body material.
Body: Cock pheasant tail fibers over a wet varnished shank.
Wings: White cock hackle tips tied vertically.
Hackle: Ginger cock.

An elegant little pattern mimicking any small dun or spinner. It should be treated with floatant and presented on the surface, leaving it to drift drag-free with the current. It is effective on a wide range of water types.

Pale Morning Dun

Dressing

Hook: TMC 100, size 14-20.
Thread: Pale yellow.
Tail: Pale blue dun hackle fibers tied forked.
Body: Pale yellow dubbing fur.
Thorax: Pale yellow dubbing fur.
Wing: Gray turkey flats.
Hackle: Light blue dun cock hackle.

This diminutive pattern is tied to suggest some of the smallest, palest colored mayfly species. It comes in to its own when trying to tempt selective trout and should always be fished on a very light leader of no more than 3lbs breaking strain. Always fish this fly drag-free.

Pale Watery

Dressing

Hook: 79704 BR, size 14-20.
Thread: Claret.
Tail: Red game hackle fibers.
Body: Pale watery green goose herl.
Wings: Two pale starling slips tied upright and separated.
Hackle: Red game cock.

Another small pattern for selective trout, it should be treated with floatant and allowed to drift free from drag with the current. A fly for rivers and streams.

Yellow Humpy

Dressing

Hook: TMC 5262, size 12.
Thread: Yellow.
Tail: See wingcase.
Body: Yellow floss.
Wings: Clipped deer hair tied vertically then separated.
Wingcase: Deer hair tied down and dressed down as tail.
Hackle: Red game cock hackle with light grizzle hackle.

Using deer hair makes the Humpy an extremely buoyant pattern designed for fishing in rough, broken water where any other fly would quickly become swamped. It is invariably fished singly on a floating line allowed to drift along with the current. It is a good fly for attracting up a fish even when there is no rise evident.

CDC Spent

Dressing

Hook: TMC 100, size 12-20.
Thread: Orange.
Tail: Blue dun hackle fibers tied forked.
Body: Rusty brown Antron.
Thorax: Rusty brown Antron.
Wing: Natural cul-de-canard tied spent.

This raggedy-looking pattern will serve as an emerging, or spent adult mayfly. Accordingly, fish on or just under the surface, either static or with the occasional twitch.

Royal Wulff

Dressing

Hook: TMC 5262, size 8-12.
Thread: Black, brown, or dark gray.
Tail: Brown deer hair.
Body: Peacock herl with a band of red floss.
Wings: Two white deer hair bunches tied upright and separated.
Hackle: Chocolate brown cock.

The Wulff range can be tied in a variety of colors. This particular version, the Royal Wulff, has the peacock herl and red floss body of other "royal" patterns. It makes a good representation of the larger mayfly species, and is at its most effective fished on a floating line during a hatch of mayfly duns.

Spent Mayfly

Dressing

Hook: TMC 5262, size 10-12.
Thread: Brown.
Tail: Three pheasant tail fibers.
Body: Cream or off-white wool.
Rib: Brown thread or floss.
Wings: Two bunches blue dun cock hackle fibers tied sloping forward and separated.
Hackle: Badger cock.

A lovely pattern for imitating a dead adult mayfly with its wings flattened in the surface film. Fish stationary, either on the surface or in the surface film.

Sherry Spinner

Dressing

Hook: 79704 BR, size 14.
Thread: Orange.
Tail: Red game hackle fibers.
Body: Orange floss.
Rib: Gold wire.
Wings: Pale starling tied spent.
Hackle: Red game cock.

This pattern provides an excellent imitation of a small stillborn dun or spinner, despite its name. It is at its most effective though fished as an imitation of the natural sherry spinner which is the imago of the blue-winged olive. Treat with floatant and fish it on the surface or in the surface film.

Bunse Green Drake

Dressing

Hook: TMC 100, size 12.
Thread: Yellow.
Tail: Two mink tail, nutria or beaver guard hairs.
Body: Green foam.
Rib: Natural dun deer hair.
Wings: Pale starling tied spent.
Hackle: Red game cock.

A useful imitation of a spent adult mayfly. The use of buoyant foam for the body means that other means of flotation, such as the hackle, can be kept sparse creating a more natural profile.

TRUE FLIES

Marabou Bloodworm

Dressing

Hook: TMC 100, size 14.
Thread: Black.
Tail: Red marabou.
Body: Red floss.
Rib: Fluorescent red silk.
Head: Peacock herl.

The larvae of some chironomid midges contain hemoglobin, which gives them a distinctive blood-red color. They live in the silt on the bottom of lakes and rivers feeding on detritus. Fish the fly deep on a floating line and a long leader or on a slow sinking line. The retrieve should be a very slow figure-of-eight with occasional short twitches to impart extra movement into the highly mobile tail.

Phantom Larva

Dressing

Hook: TMC 100, size 12-16.
Thread: Black.
Body: Underbody – silver tinsel; Overbody – stretched clear polythene.
Thorax: Orange floss.

This pattern imitates a small transparent creature which is quite active and predatory. It should be fished slowly along the bottom either on a floating line and a long leader or on an intermediate sinking line.

Phantom Pupa

Dressing

Hook: TMC 100, size 14.
Thread: Black.
Body: Yellow floss.
Rib: Flat fine silver.
Thorax: Orange ostrich.
Wingcase: Slip of pheasant tail.

This pattern is a good pupal imitation for midges and mosquitoes. It should be fished either singly or as part of a team on a floating line and long leader. The retrieve should be very slow with the line simply allowed to drift around on surface currents.

Brassie

Dressing

Hook: TMC 100, size 14-20.
Thread: Black.
Body: Copper wire.
Thorax: Peacock herl.

This simple pattern is a good imitation of a midge pupa, its slim profile and weighted body helping it to cut quickly through the surface film. On still waters it should be fished slowly on a floating line either with a steady figure-of-eight retrieve or merely allowed to drift around on the breeze. On rivers it can be cast upstream to fish which have been spotted feeding subsurface.

Hatching Midge Pupa

Dressing

Hook: TMC 100, size 12-16.
Thread: Black.
Tail: White Antron fibers.
Body: Black floss tied sparse.
Rib: Silver wire.
Thorax: Red floss.
Head: Peacock herl.
Breathing siphons: White antron floss.

A beautiful mimic of a midge pupa about to hatch, it should be fished either in the surface film or a few inches below retrieving extremely slowly. It is at its best fished on a floating line with a long leader cast across the breeze and allowed to drift around naturally. Takes are usually very confident, but gentle, with the trout picking up the fly before moving on to look for more natural midge pupae.

Carnill's Adult Buzzer (Emerger)

Dressing

Hook: TMC 100, size 12-18.
Thread: Black.
Body: Olive dubbing blend.
Rib: Silver wire.
Thorax: Mole.
Emerging wings: Two white hackle tips.

Although called an adult buzzer this pattern, developed for fishing midge hatches on lakes and reservoirs, is an effective imitation of the emerging midge. It should be fished on a floating line, either singly or as the point fly of a team. A slow steady retrieve is the most productive.

Suspender Midge

Dressing

Hook: TMC 100, size 14.
Thread: Black.
Tail: White Antron fibers.
Body: Black dubbing blend.
Rib: Gold wire.
Head: Bronze peacock herl.
Suspender ball: White plastazote in nylon stocking mesh.

This pattern imitates superbly the midge bursting free of its pupal shuck. The ball of buoyant foam at the head keeps the Suspender Midge floating in the surface film which is the exact position the trout expect to find the natural. It should be fished on a floating line, either cast in the path of rising fish or fished static in areas of trout activity.

Olive Midge (Emerger)

Dressing

Hook: TMC 100, size 12.
Thread: Pale primrose.
Body: Golden olive dubbing blend.
Rib: Yellow floss.
Wings: Two blue dun hackle points tied back over body.
Hackle: Two turns of grizzly cock hackle.

This tangled-looking fly can be used to imitate an emerging midge or caddisfly, if fished in the surface film.

Olive Midge

Dressing
Hook: TMC 3769, size 18. **Thread:** Olive. **Body:** Olive Fur. **Hackle:** Grizzly cock.

A useful dry fly to represent any very small winged insect, such as a midge. Fish on the surface without imparting any movement.

Gray Duster

Dressing
Hook: TMC 3769, size 12. **Thread:** Black. **Body:** Gray Antron. **Hackle:** Badger cock.

A bushy little dry fly which is a useful imitation of many small winged insects, including mosquitoes and midges. Treat with floatant and leave it to drift on the surface.

Reed Smut

Dressing

Hook: TMC 3769, size 18.
Thread: Black.
Body: Black seal fur.
Hackle: Grizzly cock.

A very effective imitation of an adult midge, or indeed any tiny winged insect. Treat with floatant and fish on the surface. There is no need to impart any but the slightest movement.

Double Badger

Dressing

Hook: TMC 100, size 14.
Thread: Black.
Body: Bronze peacock herl.
Wings: Two wound badger cock hackles.

Adult midges have only one biological aim: to reproduce. A mating pair on the water surface is a bonus to a trout: two for the price of one. Cast the fly onto the surface and leave it there.

Mosquito Adult

Dressing

Hook: TMC 100, size 14-20.
Thread: Black.
Body: Thinly dubbed gray polypropylene.
Rib: Black silk.
Wings: Two small grizzly hackles
tied spent.
Hackle: Blue dun cock.

This fly can be used to represent any gray-colored midge or mosquito, or even a mayfly. Fish on the surface and move only slightly, if at all.

Griffith's Gnat

Dressing

Hook: TMC 5262, size 16-20.
Thread: Black.
Body: Peacock herl.
Hackle: Grizzle cock hackle wound the entire length of the body.

This simple little fly makes a wonderful representation of a small black midge as well as a whole host of other aquatic and terrestrial insects. With such a small hook it must be fished on light tackle. A short tail of clear Antron may be added to give the pattern extra sparkle thereby changing its name to the Sparkle Gnat.

Hawthorn Fly

Dressing

Hook: TMC 100, size 12-14.
Thread: Black.
Body: Black polypropylene.
Wings: Light blue dun hackle points.
Legs: Two strands of black horsehair trailing.
Hackle: Black cock.

Adult bibionids are abundant for short periods and during their peak often fall onto the water. The adult hawthorn fly emerges during early summer where the long legged males can be seen dancing in swarms around the tops of bushes. The fly should be fished singly on a floating line where it can either be fished as a standard dry fly or allowed to sink below the surface and retrieved with a slow figure-of-eight.

Crane Fly Larva

Dressing

Hook: TMC 5262, size 8.
Thread: Brown.
Body: Underbody – wool or silk;
Overbody – yellow dyed dental latex.
Rib: Oval gold tinsel.
Hackle: Small clipped white hackle.

The larvae (leatherjackets) of some crane flies are aquatic or semiaquatic, living in the mud at the bottom and sides of the water. Having no legs they do not move far or fast (although some species can swim by flattening the body). Fish very slowly along the bottom, close to the water margins.

Daddy-longlegs (Walker Pattern)

Dressing

Hook: TMC 5262, size 10.
Thread: Brown.
Body: Varnished natural raffia.
Wings: Four chinchilla grizzle hackles tied spent.
Legs: Eight pheasant tail fibers each with two knots.
Hackle: Two long red game fiber hackles.

This is a wonderful imitation of a crane fly. These insects emerge in large numbers and get blown onto the water or land there by accident, where they quickly drown. Fish either on the surface or let it sink below as if waterlogged. Works well either fished static or with a steady retrieve.

Orvis Crane Fly

Dressing

Hook: TMC 100, size 14.
Thread: Black.
Body: Yellow or orange floss.
Hackle: Long black cock.

A simple but effective imitation of an orange or yellow colored crane fly adult. Fish on the surface or in the surface film to represent either a dead or drowning insect.

Wet Daddy

Dressing

Hook: TMC 5262, size 8.
Thread: Black.
Body: Natural raffia.
Rib: Fine gold wire.
Semi-hackle: Light red-brown cock palmered halfway down body to look like legs (optional).
Hackle: Long brown partridge fibers under golden pheasant tippet.

A great fly for windy lakes, fished as the top dropper of a three fly team. This bushy, brightly colored fly is a "change" pattern when the trout are taking natural daddy-longlegs but are proving difficult to tempt on conventional imitations. Fish it at a steady pace lifting the rod top at the end of the retrieve to work the fly in the surface.

Detached Body Crane Fly

Dressing

Hook: TMC 100, size 10.
Thread: Brown.
Tail: Elk or deer hair detached and bound with white thread.
Wings: Two chinchilla grizzly tied spent.
Legs: Six pheasant tail fibers knotted twice.
Hackle: Two red game cock tied long.

This pattern uses a detached body of deer hair to provide extra buoyancy. This, and the correspondingly small hook, help the pattern to float well even in very rough conditions. Fish it on a floating line and allow it to drift along in the surface film.

Grafham Drone

Dressing

Hook: TMC 100, size 14.
Thread: Black.
Body: Yellow floss.
Rib: Black thread.
Wings: Bunch of blue dun hackle fibers.
Hackle: Red game cock hackle tied short.

Although this pattern appears to imitate a drone fly, an insect which resembles a honey bee, it actually imitates a hover fly, a much smaller insect with distinct black and yellow bands. Fish it right in the surface film just as the natural would sit.

Drone Fly

Dressing

Hook: TMC 100, size 14.
Thread: Red.
Body: Wound yellow ostrich herl.
Rib: Black ostrich herl.
Wings: Two white hackle tips.
Hackle: Natural red game cock.

Another misnamed pattern, this imitation of the terrestrial hover fly is most effective during mid-summer when the naturals are at their peak. Fish on a floating line clipping off the hackle fibers beneath the hook to help it sit low in the surface.

True Flies

Bluebottle

Dressing

Hook: TMC 100, size 12-14.
Thread: Black.
Body: Blue flashback wrapped with black ostrich herl.
Wings: Two blue dun hackle points tied flat.
Hackle: Black cock.

Although designed to imitate a bluebottle, this pattern is effective when other dark terrestrials, such as beetles, are on the water. It may be fished in the surface film by applying floatant or left to sink, where the retrieve should be slow.

Black Gnat

Dressing

Hook: TMC 100, size 12-20.
Thread: Black.
Tail: Black cock hackle fibers.
Body: Black wool.
Wing: Paired slips of gray mallard primary.
Hackle: Dyed black cock.

This pattern imitates various, similar species of terrestrials known as black gnats. It should be fished on a floating line and allowed simply to drift on the surface without added movement.

CADDISFLIES

Caddis Larva

Dressing

Hook: TMC 5262, size 10.
Thread: Black.
Body: Dubbed hare's ear.
Rib: Fine gold wire.
Thorax: White floss or silk.
Hackle: Short black hen.

Caddis larva live on the bottom and move only slowly. Fish the fly deep and retrieve smoothly either with a series of short draws or with a steady figure-of-eight. To get the fly to fish along the bottom it may be weighted and used on a floating line and a long leader.

Cased Caddis

Dressing

Hook: TMC 800 or TMC 5262, size 6-12.
Thread: Brown.
Body: Underbody of wool with medium grains of gravel stuck to wet epoxy adhesive and dried.
Thorax: White ostrich herl.
Hackle: Black hen.

This is a particularly lifelike imitation of those caddisfly larvae, which incorporate gravel in their "case." Other items such as small pieces of stick can also be used to represent other species. Fish the pattern very slowly and smoothly along the bottom.

Stickfly

Dressing

Hook: TMC 5262, size 10.
Thread: Brown.
Body: Pheasant tail.
Rib: Copper wire.
Thorax: Fluorescent yellow floss.
Hackle: Short red game cock.

Another well-tried imitation of a caddis larva, to be fished very slowly along the bottom.

Green Tag Stickfly

Dressing

Hook: TMC 100, size 12.
Thread: Brown.
Tag: Fluorescent green floss.
Body: Bronze peacock herl.
Hackle: Dark red game.

As an early season pattern it works best fished slowly along the bottom. It is also effective fished on the point of a three fly team working the flies at various levels.

Longhorns

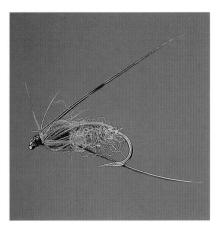

Dressing

Hook: TMC 100, size 12.
Thread: Black.
Body: Amber dubbing on first two thirds with dark brown on last third.
Wingcase: Pheasant tail fibers tied back.
Antennae: Two pheasant tail fibers.
Hackle: Short red game.

A marvelous imitation of a caddis pupa, with its long antennae. Caddis pupae rise rapidly to the surface when ready to emerge. Fish the pattern in the surface film, retrieving in short sharp pulls to imitate the struggle to escape from the pupal shuck. Be ready for savage takes.

Green DF Partridge

Dressing

Hook: TMC 100, size 12.
Thread: Black.
Body: Fluorescent green floss.
Rib: Fine oval silver tinsel.
Hackle and legs: Partridge hackle.

Another pattern which can be used as a mimic of a caddis pupa. Vary the color of tying and keep a selection of brown, black, yellow, and green versions. Fish either in the surface film or, using a floating line, allow to sink and then retrieve, as if it is heading to the surface to emerge.

Bead Head Emerging Caddis

Dressing

Hook: TMC 3761, size 10-14.
Thread: Gray.
Tail: A few strands of Sparkle Yarn.
Underbody: Gray fur and brown Sparkle Yarn mixed.
Overbody: Gray Sparkle Yarn pulled loosely over the body.
Wing: A few strands of gray deer hair.
Thorax: Peacock herl.
Head: Gold bead.

This pattern is a deadly imitation of a caddis pupa, which should be fished quickly mimicking the pupa rising to the surface. The gold bead at the head provides weight, helping the fly to sink quickly, along with a wonderful sparkle suggesting the gases trapped within the pupal skin.

Elk Hair Caddis

Dressing

Hook: TMC 100, size 10-18.
Thread: Tan.
Body: Hare's fur either natural or dyed olive or black ribbed with fine gold wire.
Hackle: Brown cock hackle wound over body.
Wing: Bleached elk hair.

This pattern is an excellent imitation of an adult caddis-fly. Fish as for the Black Sedge. The buoyancy of the elk hair makes this pattern particularly effective in rough or broken water.

Black Sedge

Dressing

Hook: TMC 100, size 10.
Thread: Black.
Body: Black wool or chenille.
Wings: Black deer or elk hair tied flat and cut square.
Hackle: Black cock tied to slope forward.

Mated females of most species oviposit directly into the water by skimming over the surface. This fly pattern can be used to represent this behavior. Treat it with floatant, cast it onto the surface and leave it sit for a while. Then pull the fly across the water so that it accelerates, covering a yard or so in about three seconds. Let it rest again (take-off aborted) and repeat the retrieve. Be ready for some explosive takes.

Large Brown Sedge

Dressing

Hook: TMC 5262, size 10.
Thread: Orange.
Tag: Yellow fluorescent floss.
Body: Clipped chestnut ostrich herl.
Wings: Bunch of red game hackles tied flat over back.
Hackle: Red game cock.

This pattern is a great imitation of the larger sedge species normally seen on the wing during dusk. It should be fished on a floating line either cast at rising fish or left to drift in areas of activity. Skating this fly can bring about a dramatic take.

Grannom

Dressing

Hook: 79704 BR, size 16.
Thread: Green.
Tag: Fluorescent green wool.
Body: Gray goose herl.
Wings: Blue dun cock fibers.
Hackle: Ginger cock.

A very effective imitation of smaller, rusty brown caddis species. Fish dry, interspersing periods of quiet drift with the occasional lift of the rod top to skate the fly across the surface.

Stocking Sedge

Dressing

Hook: TMC 100, size 14-18.
Thread: Brown.
Body: Yellow wool with a brown cock hackle wound over.
Wing: Light mottled turkey tail stuck to a sheet of stocking mesh and then cut to shape.
Hackle: Brown cock hackle tied full.
Antennae: Two cock pheasant tail fibers.

An excellent imitation of an adult caddis with long antennae, it should be fished with the standard technique for patterns of this type. The method of sticking mottled turkey tail to stocking mesh gives the wing a very lifelike profile and makes it very robust.

Pale Sedge

Dressing

Hook: TMC 100, size 10.
Thread: Brown.
Body: Cinnamon turkey tail.
Rib: Gold twist.
Wings: Natural hen pheasant wing fibers rolled and tied flat.
Hackle: Ginger cock at head and palmered ginger cock over body.

Very usefully employed as a caddis adult resting on the surface prior to taking flight. Leave it drift with the current and every now and then skate it across the surface for about a couple of feet.

Cinnamon Sedge

Dressing

Hook: TMC 100, size 10.
Thread: Black.
Body: Brown pheasant tail fibers.
Wings: Cinnamon turkey quill.
Hackle: Ginger or natural red cock.

A standard pattern for imitating reddish-brown caddis adults sitting on the surface. Treat with floatant and let the fly drift along and occasionally pull to indicate the insect accelerating before takeoff.

Caperer

Dressing

Hook: TMC 100, size 14.
Thread: Orange.
Body: Mixed orange and fiery-brown dubbing blend.
Rib: Fine gold wire.
Wings: Red game cock hackles tied back.
Hackle: Red game cock.

Use to imitate an adult caddis fluttering along the surface, either laying eggs or about to take flight.

G & H Sedge

Dressing

Hook: TMC 5262, size 10.
Thread: Brown.
Body: Bright green dubbing strung from bend to head.
Wings: Spun deer hair shaped to form roof-shaped wings.
Antennae: Stripped red game cock hackle stalks.
Hackle: Red game cock.

The use of deer body hair clipped to shape gives this pattern a very lifelike profile along with making it extremely buoyant. It should be fished on the surface, the natural buoyancy of the deer hair making it very easy to skate without becoming waterlogged.

STONEFLIES

Stonefly Nymph

Dressing

Hook: TMC 100, size 12.
Thread: Black.
Tail: Two fibers besom.
Body: Stripped peacock herl.
Thorax: Peacock herl.
Wingcase: Dark grouse herl.
Hackle: Grouse breast feather.

The nymphs of most stonefly species creep along the bottom feeding on algae and detritus. If disturbed they will simply drift with the current until they sink back to the bottom. For this reason, on rivers, stonefly nymph imitations are most effective cast upstream and allowed to sink as they are swept along with the current. On lakes, a slow steady retrieve is the most productive.

Yellow Sally (wet)

Dressing

Hook: TMC 100, size 14-16.
Thread: Primrose.
Body: Dubbed pale yellow wool.
Hackle: Yellow cock hackle.

A wet version of the Yellow Sally which may be used to imitate an egg laying or spent adult. It should be fished on a floating line close to the surface either upstream or using the standard wet fly technique of down-and-across.

Willow Fly

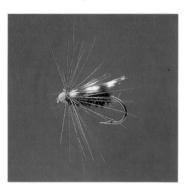

Dressing

Hook: TMC 100, size 14-16.
Thread: Orange.
Body: Bronze peacock herl.
Wings: Two small medium grizzle hackles tied flat over back.
Hackle: Brown dun cock.

Although the Willow Fly was developed to imitate one particular species of stonefly it is equally effective suggesting a whole range of small dark stonefly species. Fish it as a standard dry fly, allowing it to drift naturally with the current.

Stonefly Adult

Dressing

Hook: TMC 5262, size 10.
Thread: Black.
Body: Dark dyed olive hare's mask fur.
Rib: Yellow silk.
Wings: Dark hen pheasant tail fibers rolled and tied down close to back and beyond the hook bend.
Hackle: Dyed olive grizzly cock.

This pattern can be used to mimic larger species of stonefly. Treat with floatant and fish on the surface. Apart from allowing the fly to drift, it is worth attempting to imitate egg-laying and taking off by moving the fly across the surface for distances of up to a yard. Take into account that stonefly adults are not particularly elegant or fast in their movements, so attempted takeoff will be slow and clumsy.

DAMSELFLIES AND DRAGONFLIES

Damselfly Nymph

Dressing

Hook: TMC 5262, size 10-12.
Thread: Olive.
Tail: Olive marabou.
Body: Olive goose.
Rib: Fine gold oval.
Thorax: Olive ostrich herl.
Wingcase: Olive goose.
Eyes: ½in brass chain links.

At times when adults are emerging, the nymphs that are ready to do so will swim up to the surface where they climb out onto reeds and sticks to shed their shuck. It then pays to fish the nymph on a floating line, letting it sink two or three feet before retrieving smoothly so that the fly lifts up in the water toward the surface.

Green Mountain Damsel

Dressing

Hook: TMC 300, size 10.
Thread: Olive.
Tail: Three goose biots dyed olive.
Body: Green Antron.
Rib: Fine gold wire.
Wingcase: Olive marabou fibers tied upright.

Another good damselfly nymph mimic, which has plenty of movement in the marabou wingcases. Fish deep or just under the surface with a steady figure-of-eight retrieve.

Cactus Damsel

Dressing

Hook: TMC 300, size 10-12.
Thread: Olive.
Tail: Olive marabou.
Body: Cactus olive chenille.
Head: ½in gold bead.

A deadly modern pattern which sparkles and undulates when retrieved. Use as other damselfly nymph imitations.

Damsel Wiggle Nymph

Dressing

Hook 1: TMC 100, size 8-10.
Thread: Tan or olive waxed nylon.
Tail: Olive or golden brown marabou fibers.
Body: Brown or olive dubbing.
Rib: Gold oval tinsel.
Hook 2: TMC 100, size 10; weighted with lead wire and linked to hook 1.
Thorax: Brown dubbing blend.
Wingcase: Brown turkey dyed olive.
Hackle: Partridge dyed olive.

Another solution to imitating the swimming action of a damselfly nymph is provided by this pattern. Here the abdomen is a separate hook linked in tandem by wire to the anterior hook which represents the head and thorax. Fish as for other damsel nymphs, either along the bottom or swimming up to the surface as if about to crawl ashore to transpose.

The Dragon

Dressing

Hook: TMC 5262, size 12.
Thread: Olive.
Tail: Three goose biots dyed olive.
Body: Olive green dubbing blend.
Rib: Olive floss.
Hackle: Brown partridge.
Head: Peacock herl.

The nymphs of these insects swim by ejecting water from their rectum. Accordingly, move the fly slowly along the bottom, but then at intervals tug the line to produce a short 6 inch explosive burst of movement, as would occur were the insect escaping from a trout.

Blue Damselfly Adult

Dressing

Hook: TMC 100, size 10.
Thread: Black.
Body: Floating fly line ribbed with black silk and varnished.
Wings: Two pairs black cock hackles tied spent.
Hackle: Blue dun.
Eyes: Plastazote balls wrapped in white tights tied in figure-of-eights.

A lifelike imitation of an adult blue damselfly. Use when adults are flying, and fish floating on the surface to imitate either a dead (spent) insect, or one in its last throes.

CRUSTACEANS

Shrimp (Scud)

Dressing

Hook: TMC 2487, or Yorkshire sedge hook, size 10-16.
Thread: Olive.
Back: Clear polyethylene or Shellback material.
Rib: Gold wire or oval.
Body hackle: Olive or orange hen or cock.

Freshwater shrimp or scud imitations should be fished close to the bottom and around weed beds where the naturals are to be found. On rivers this can mean casting the fly well upstream of a fish to allow the fly plenty of time to sink to the correct level. On still waters a floating line, a long leader and a slow, steady retrieve is the most effective technique.

Crayfish

Red Spot Shrimp

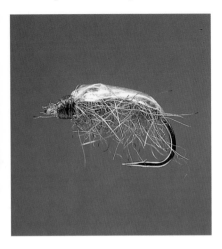

Dressing

Hook: Yorkshire sedge hook, size 10.
Thread: Waxed olive.
Body: Underbody – fine lead wire; Overbody – red wool with an equal amount of olive Mohair and dubbing tied at right angles to the center of the shank/wool clipped to make spots at sides of body.
Back: Two layers of clear plastic sheet.
Rib: Gold wire.
Legs: Olive body fibers picked out.

Water shrimps (scuds) are parasitized by worms which cause them to develop red spots on their body and also to change their behavior. Instead of crawling around and remaining out of sight, the parasitized animals repeatedly jump up from the bottom, so attracting the attention of fish and ensuring that they are eaten. Imitate this behavior by using a floating line, letting the fly sink to the bottom, and retrieving it in short twitches between each of you which allow the fly to sink back to the bottom.

Dressing

Hook: TMC 300, size 4-8.
Thread: Olive.
Tail and back: Yellow shellback over olive Twinkle.
Body: Palmered dyed saddle hackle.
Rib: Flat Mylar medium.
Antennae and mouthparts: Dyed elk hair.
Eyes: Black plastic beads.
Claws: Two pairs of short, dyed grizzle saddle hackles from the densest part of the hackle.

This is a beautiful imitation of a freshwater crayfish. Fish along the bottom, moving the fly along smoothly to imitate the animal walking along. Every now and then shoot it backward by tugging hard on the line, after which it can be retrieved for a few yards in a series of short tugs.

MISCELLANEOUS INSECTS AND ORGANISMS

Peter Gathercole's Waterlouse

Dressing

Hook: TMC 100, size 12-16.
Thread: Black or brown.
Back: Gray-brown feather fibers.
Tail: Some back fibers sticking out.
Body: Gray rabbit fur with a short-fibered partridge hackle over back.
Rib: Silver wire.
Antennae: Two brown feather fibers.

Waterlice (hoglice) crawl around the bottom of lakes and slow-moving rivers. Fish this imitation slowly on a sinking or a floating line and long leader, using a figure-of-eight retrieve.

Corixa

Dressing

Hook: TMC 100, size 10-14.
Thread: Brown.
Tag: Silver tinsel or Mylar.
Body: Underbody – lead foil covered with dirty-white or pale lemon yellow angora wool dubbing; overbody – pale orange raffia stretched over back and streaked with brown.
Rib: Fine silver wire.
Hackle: Two bunches of brown hen fibers.

Corixids (water boatmen) either swim along the bottom among submerged vegetation, or else up to and down from the surface to collect bubbles of air. Both activities can be imitated with this weighted pattern.

Large Brown Corixa and Plastazote Corixa

Dressing

Hook: TMC 100, size 10-12.
Thread: Black.
Tag: Silver tinsel.
Body: White floss or Plastazote.
Rib: Flat silver wire.
Wingcase: Pheasant tail fibers (bad side).
Head: Black thread.
Legs: Two goose biots.

These patterns are buoyant (especially the Plastazote) and are especially good for representing water boatmen swimming along the surface collecting air. When using a sinking line it is possible to imitate a corixid diving back to the bottom with its air bubble by ceasing the retrieve.

Quick Sight Beetle

Dressing

Hook: TMC 100, size 12-16.
Thread: Black.
Body: Black closed cell foam with a spot of fluorescent orange paint to aid visibility.
Legs: Thick black thread.
Head: Black closed cell foam.

When they land on the water terrestrial beetles sit very low in the surface. This imitation uses buoyant foam and is designed to fish right in the surface film, just like the natural insect. To help the angler see the fly at range a spot of fluorescent paint is applied to the thorax. On rivers this pattern should be cast upstream and allowed to free-drift. On still waters it should be fished static.

Letort Cricket

Dressing

Hook: TMC 100, size 12.
Thread: Black.
Body: Black chenille.
Wings: Black goose tied flat over body.
Head: Clipped black deer.

If takes are not forthcoming, it is a good idea to cast this imitation so that it causes a definite "plop". When the natural lands on the water it creates quite a disturbance. This acts as a trigger often causing a fish to rush up and grab the fly. A happy coincidence is that cricket and grasshopper imitations prove very tempting to larger trout.

Dave's Hopper

Dressing

Hook: TMC 5263, size 8-12.
Thread: Brown.
Tail: Red calf tail.
Body: Yellow polypropylene yarn with a brown cock hackle wound over and clipped short.
Legs: Two slips of brown turkey fibers each knotted once.
Wing: Mottled brown turkey.
Head: Deer hair spun and clipped to shape.

A very effective pattern which can be used to imitate grasshoppers. Employ a kick-swimming retrieve pattern. Making the fly land with a "plop" will often induce a fish into grabbing it.

Grasshopper

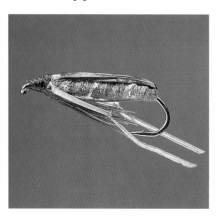

Dressing

Hook: TMC 300, size 8.
Thread: Brown.
Body: Green polyethylene foam or Plastazote below, with brown raffine or pheasant tail fibers tied over the top to represent wings.
Legs: Two swan primary feather fibers dyed medium-brown.
Hackle: Beard hackle of 8–10 pheasant tail fibers tied short.

A lifelike imitation of a field grasshopper, which should be fished as other Orthoptera patterns by retrieving across the surface with short tugs to indicate kick-swimming.

Floating Fry

Dressing

Hook: TMC 300, size 6-10.
Thread: White for first part then black to finish.
Body: Underbody – fish-shaped tube of Plastazote with a red floss lateral line and throat; Overbody – pearl Mylar tubing.
Back and tail: Peacock herl interspersed with black Twinkle.
Head: Black thread built up to proportion.
Eye: Self-adhesive decal covered in epoxy resin.

Either fish this static pattern on a floating line to represent a stunned or dead fish, or fish it on a sinking line so that it swims along above the bottom, alternatively rising and diving when the line is retrieved in short sharp draws or swimming parallel to the bottom if retrieved smoothly.

Perch Fry

Dressing

Hook: TMC 300, size 8.
Thread: Black.
Body: Gold tinsel with two short, dyed grizzle saddle hackles tied in behind head.
Tail: Golden pheasant tippets.
Beard hackle: Red cock.

This pattern provides an authentic representation of a small perch. Fish so that it swims close to weeds and other submerged vegetation.

Zonker

Dressing

Hook: TMC 300, size 8.
Thread: Black.
Body: Silver Mylar dressed over wool gray rabbit Zonker strip tied in at tail and head and glued to body.
Beard hackle: Yellow cock.

A lively imitation of a small fish which is best fished either deep or in midwater (depending on where the real bait fish are lying). Retrieve either smoothly or to mimic the darting escape of a small fish. The Zonker strip wiggles and undulates realistically when wet.

Polystickle

Dressing

Hook: TMC 300, size 6.
Thread: Black.
Back and tail: Brown orange or yellow raffine.
Body: Black silk wound on to a silvered hook and crimson floss wound on to hook at front end. Body then built into fish shape with polyethylene.
Head: Varnished tying silk.
Beard hackle: Red or orange hackle fibers.

Another excellent minnow or other small fish imitation. It is most effective fished on a slow or medium-fast sinking line around weed beds and other structures where bait fish congregate.

Leech (Poodle)

Dressing

Hook: TMC 300, size 6.
Thread: Black.
Tail: Black marabou.
Tag: Two or three turns of black wool.
Body: Black chenille.
Body plumes: Four or five small shuttle-cocks of black marabou tied along top of shank.

Leeches swim by undulating their body up and down, a movement which is captured perfectly by the marabou plumes and tail in this pattern. Fish along the bottom, retrieving in short 6 inch pulls or a figure-of-eight retrieve.

Miscellaneous Insects and Organisms

Floating Snail

Dressing

Hook: TMC 100, size 10.
Thread: Black.
Body: Black or brown chenille wound into a ball.

Aquatic snails of various species live on the bottom, among submerged vegetation, and suspended upside down from the surface film where they eat floating weed and algae. This pattern represents the last of these and should be fished in the surface film. Move the artificial fly very slowly.

Swannundaze Alder Larva

Dressing

Hook: TMC 5262, size 10.
Thread: Brown.
Tail: Red game hackles.
Body: Underbody – silver flat tinsel; Overbody – Swannundaze.
Thorax: Orange seal fur.
Wingcase: Pheasant tail.
Hackle: Gray partridge.

A useful imitation of the voracious alderfly larva. The translucent abdomen is particularly effective. Fish the pattern slowly along the bottom either on a sinking line or a floating line and a long leader.

Black Palmer

Dressing

Hook: TMC 100, size 12.
Thread: Black.
Body: Black dubbing blend.
Rib: Silver wire.
Hackle: Black hen or cock palmered.

This pattern can be used to imitate a dead or emerging alderfly when fished in the surface film or near the surface, or if wound with a stiff cock hackle, an adult sitting on the water. Either leave it to float with the current or impart appropriate movement (as for a stonefly or mayfly adult).

Adult Alderfly

Dressing

Hook: TMC 100, size 12.
Thread: Black.
Body: Black goose.
Wings: Paired grouse tied back wet-style.
Hackle: Black hen.

This is a wet fly pattern designed to imitate the adult alderfly. On rivers it should be fished down-and-across on a floating line and on still waters in a series of short, slow draws.

Black Ant

Dressing

Hook: TMC 100, size 14.
Thread: Black.
Body: Black acetate floss.
Wings: Two blue dun hackle tips tied over back.
Hackle: Black cock behind head built up from floss.

Winged ants are extremely abundant for short periods, usually during summer after rain. If good numbers fall on to the water's surface they can provoke the trout into frenzied feeding. Fish this pattern on a floating line applying a small amount of floatant so that it sits low, right in the surface film.

Ghost Swift Moth

Dressing

Hook: TMC 5262, size 8.
Thread: White.
Body: Cream ostrich herl.
Rib: Stiff cream-colored cock hackle.
Wings: Swan secondary wing feathers.
Hackle: Cream and pale ginger cock hackle.

Although the natural ghost swift moth is actually so rare that you are unlikely to encounter it, this pattern makes a great imitation of a whole range of large, pale moths. It is at its most effective fished from dusk into dark, the time the naturals are on the wing.

Bee

Dressing

Hook: TMC 9300, size 10.
Thread: Black.
Body: Banded yellow black and white ostrich herl.
Wings: Two grizzly hackle points.
Legs: Four dyed black pheasant tail fibers.

Bees and bumblebees are not accomplished swimmers. When they end up on water they drown. Cast the fly onto the water so that it splashes down and jiggle it slightly as it drifts along.

Hoolet

Dressing

Hook: TMC 100, size 10.
Thread: Black.
Body: Cork strip with peacock herl wound over.
Wings: Cinnamon turkey.
Hackle: Two natural red cock hackles.

This pattern is usefully employed at dusk to represent any of the thousands of species of medium-sized brown moths that might fall on the water.

Black Moth

Dressing

Hook: TMC 100, size 10.
Thread: Black.
Body: Black polypropylene.
Thorax: Orange fluorescent floss.
Wings: Black hen hackle tips.
Hackle: Black cock.

Use as for other moth patterns. The same pattern could also represent a black caddisfly, in which case more movement could validly be imparted to the fly.

NON-IMITATIVE PATTERNS

Not all fly patterns are designed to mimic specific insects or, for that matter, other creatures likely to be taken by the trout. In fact, the majority of trout flies are far more general, intended to induce the fish into taking them either out of inquisitiveness or sheer aggression.

ABOVE: A fine brown trout taken on a dry fly.

A large proportion of the trout's feeding strategy is non-specific. Trout are opportunistic feeders and if there is no definite hatch or fall of insects then they are likely to take anything which they presume to be edible.

Trout flies fall into four main groups: dry flies, wet flies, nymphs and bugs and streamers and hairwings.

DRY FLIES

As their name suggests, dry flies are intended not to sink but to float on the water's surface. It is this group which includes all the imitations of the adult aquatic insects, such as the caddisflies, mayflies, Chironomid midges and stoneflies along with many terrestrial invertebrates.

Many dry flies are designed to imitate specific types or even species of insects. Typical examples include the Blue Winged Olive and the Hawthorn Fly both of which are tied to fool trout which are feeding selectively on the real thing. Conversely patterns like the Claret Hopper and the Hare's Ear are tied not with a specific creature in mind, but to offer the trout something with the size and profile of something which might be alive and edible.

WET FLIES

Wet flies as a group are almost all designed with this random feeding in mind. There are a few notable exceptions such as the wet Mayfly imitations developed on the giant limestone loughs of Ireland, but by and large this very traditional group contains flies with a wide variety of shapes and colors, some dark and bushy others slim and brightly

colored along with every conceivable variation between.

NYMPHS AND BUGS

This is a large catch-all group encompassing all those patterns which suggest something relatively lifelike. They can be imitative, as in the case of the freshwater shrimp or alderfly larva, or more impressionistic such as the Teeny Nymph or the Colonel's Creeper.

Much of the aquatic fauna on which trout prey are well camouflaged to blend in with their environment of weed, sand or mud. To this end many nymphs and bugs are tied with subtle, natural hued materials: various shades of brown and olive are particular favorites.

STREAMERS AND HAIRWINGS

Also known as lures, streamer and hairwing patterns are usually quite large and most often tied on longshank hooks either singly or in tandem. The wing is normally at least as long as the hook and often a good deal longer to give the fly plenty of movement in the water. For this reason the winging materials are usually soft and mobile particularly in the case of streamers which often use feathers such as cock hackles or marabou. Today, hairwings are less

ABOVE: Lures, streamers and hairwings tend to be used in rivers where the current will give plenty of movement.

popular than they were and tend to be used in rivers where the current already gives them plenty of action.

Within this group some patterns fulfil an imitative role as mimics of small fish, leeches and larger invertebrates such as crayfish. More often they are tied to induce the trout into taking them out of aggression or pure inquisitiveness.

Among the more imitative patterns are those such as the Perch Fry and the Zonker designed to imitate small bait fish. Others mimic something alive and potentially edible and include such patterns as the Olive Tadpole and the Woolly Bugger which suggest anything from a damselfly or dragonfly nymph to a leech.

However, it is as attractors that lures are probably best known. Tied on large longshank hooks they come in a wide range of colors from black and white, to red, yellow, pink, and even orange. They are all designed, not to fool the fish into taking them as food, but as something which excites their aggression or inquisitiveness.

LEFT: Changing fly. Seeking to induce the trout's inquisitiveness.

DRY FLIES

Claret Hopper

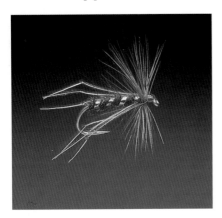

Dressing

Hook: TMC 100, size 10.
Thread: Brown.
Body: Claret Antron.
Rib: Pearl Lurex.
Legs: Knotted fibers of cock pheasant tail.
Hackle: Natural red cock hackle.

The Hopper is a general but deadly fly for still water trout. The legs of knotted pheasant tail fibers give the pattern a wonderful "buzz" making it look like an insect trapped in the surface film. It should be fished either singly or as part of a team on a floating line. It is at its most effective when sitting right in the water's surface rather than on it.

Black Bi-visible

Dressing

Hook: TMC 100, size 8-14.
Thread: Black.
Tail: Black cock hackle tip.
Body hackle: Black cock hackles.
Collar hackle: A white cock hackle.

A bushy fly, using closely wound cock hackles along the entire length of the hook shank to produce a ultra-high floating pattern. It may be used on rivers as a general attractor or to mimic small dark terrestrials such as the black gnat or hawthorn fly. It also makes a passable representation of the darker species of caddis fly.

Hare's Ear

Dressing

Hook: TMC 100, size 14-18.
Thread: Brown.
Tail: Hare's fur.
Body: Fur from hare's ear.
Rib: Fine flat gold tinsel.
Wing: Gray starling.
Hackle: Hare's fur picked out with a needle.

The mottled brown of the hare's fur gives this pattern the advantage of looking like nothing in particular while, at the same time, having the appearance of something alive and potentially edible. The Hare's Ear is a tremendously versatile pattern which will take fish in a wide range of conditions and water types.

Wickham's Fancy

Dressing

Hook: TMC 100, size 14-18.
Thread: Brown.
Tail: Natural red game cock hackle fibers.
Body: Flat gold tinsel.
Rib: Gold wire.
Body hackle: Natural red game cock.
Wing: Starling primary.
Hackle: Natural red game cock.

Superficially, the Wickham's Fancy has the general profile of a sedge or caddis fly; it is far more versatile making a superb pattern to try when fish are feeding on nothing in particular, the glint of gold shining through the "buzz" of a palmered hackle.

WET FLIES

Zulu

Dressing

Hook: TMC 100, size 12-8.
Thread: Black.
Tail: Red wool.
Body: Black Antron.
Rib: Flat silver tinsel.
Hackle: Black cock hackle.

A great fly for a big wave, the Zulu is particularly effective on large natural lakes. Usually fished on the top dropper as part of a three fly team on a floating fly line. This "bob fly" position allows the Zulu to be worked in the wave by gently lifting the rod top at the end of the retrieve.

Soldier Palmer

Dressing

Hook: TMC 100, size 14-10.
Thread: Brown.
Tail: Red wool.
Body: Red wool.
Rib: Fine gold tinsel.
Hackle: Natural red game cock hackle.

This bright fly, which can be tied even brighter using fluorescent red wool, is effective when fished on any position on the leader; in fact some anglers even use three Soldier Palmers at the same time! Usually fished with a quick retrieve, even stripping the line if the trout are in the mood for the chase.

Butcher

Dressing

Hook: TMC 100, size 14-8.
Thread: Black.
Tail: Red goose.
Body: Flat silver tinsel.
Rib: Fine oval silver tinsel.
Wing: Blue mallard.
Hackle: Black cock hackle.

Although regarded as a general attractor, the flash silver and the dark mallard wing can suggest the natural shading of a small fish. The silver body can also suggest the trapped gases in the skin of an emerging nymph and to this end some anglers trim the fly's wing and tail to short stubs producing the Butcher Nymph.

Mallard and Claret

Dressing

Hook: TMC 100, size 14-10.
Thread: Black.
Tail: Golden pheasant tippet strands.
Body: Claret dubbing.
Rib: Fine, oval gold tinsel.
Wing: Bronze mallard.
Hackle: Brown cock hackle.

A fine fly for the point or middle dropper of a three fly team, the Mallard and Claret is equally effective on river and still water. It is a subtly colored fly at its best in overcast conditions where the rich claret of the body is set off beautifully by the golden rib and the bright orange of the golden pheasant tippet tail.

NYMPHS

Montana

Dressing

Hook: TMC 300, size 8-12.
Thread: Black.
Tail: Black cock hackle fibers.
Underbody: Lead wire.
Body: Black chenille.
Thorax: Fluorescent green chenille.
Thorax cover: Black chenille.
Hackle: Black cock hackle.

Although originally designed to imitate a stonefly nymph the Montana has taken on a much more general role. It is effective fished either dead drift or down-and-across on rivers. On still waters it is a great early season pattern fished slowly along the lake bed either on a fast sinking or intermediate line.

Teeny Nymph

Dressing

Hook: TMC 100, size 6-12.
Thread: Olive.
Body: Dyed olive pheasant tail fibers.
Hackle: Dyed olive pheasant tail fibers.

Jim Teeny of Portland, Oregon designed this nymph to catch trout, steelhead, and Pacific salmon. Tied in a wide range of colors and sizes, when used for trout the more natural hues such as black, brown, and olive are usually the most effective. The Teeny Nymph is quick, easy and cheap to tie making it perfect for fishing rocky, fast flowing rivers.

Colonel's Creeper

Dressing

Hook: TMC 300, size 6-8.
Thread: Brown.
Underbody: Lead wire.
Tail: Hare's guard hairs.
Body: Natural hare's fur.
Rib: Clear nymph glass.
Wingcases: Cock pheasant body feathers.
Legs: Gray goose biots.

This heavily weighted pattern is designed to tempt big trout feeding close to the bottom. Designed by a Colonel Unwin of Kenya it should be fished either on a floating line and a long leader or on a slow sinking line when casting into deeper water. With a bent hook shank and a weighted underbody, it fishes upside down. This prevents the fly from snagging bottom weed.

Lead Bug

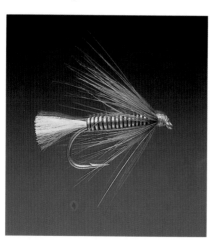

Dressing

Hook: TMC 100, size 10-12.
Thread: Olive.
Tail: Olive floss.
Body: Lead wire.
Hackle: Olive hen hackle.

This heavyweight fly, consisting almost entirely of lead wire, is designed to sink quickly when used to target trout in clear water. On rivers and on still waters the trick is to predict the trout's route and to place the fly far enough in front so that it has sunk to the correct depth by the time the trout reaches the spot.

Cat's Whisker

Dressing

Hook: TMC 300, size 6-10.
Thread: Black.
Tail: White marabou.
Body: Fluorescent lime green chenille.
Wing: White marabou.
Eyes: Silver chain bead.

The combination of the fluorescent lime green body and the mobility of the marabou wing and tail make the Cat's Whisker among the most deadly of still water lures. It is successful throughout the season, usually fished on a slow or fast sinking line. The retrieve should be varied from a series of short, steady draws to a fast strip, inducing the trout into grabbing the fly out of aggression.

Whisky Fly

Dressing

Hook: TMC 300, size 6-10.
Thread: Fluorescent orange.
Body: Flat gold tinsel.
Rib: Fluorescent orange floss.
Wing: Orange squirrel tail.
Hackle: Orange cock hackle.

This gaudy fly is one for high summer when the rainbow trout are at their most aggressive. On the larger still waters *Daphnia*, a small animal plankton, makes up an important part of the trout's diet. Although individual *Daphnia* are far too small to imitate effectively, trout which are feeding on them will take a brightly colored lure.

Olive Tadpole

Dressing

Hook: TMC 100, size 8-10.
Thread: Olive.
Tail: Olive marabou.
Underbody: Lead wire.
Body: Olive chenille.
Rib: Fine gold wire.
Hackle: Gray partridge, dyed olive.

Though often regarded as a general representation of a damsel nymph, the Olive Tadpole is just as deadly even when trout are not taking the naturals. It is at its best fished either on an intermediate sinking or a floating line with a long leader. Either way the retrieve should vary from a figure-of-eight to short steady draws.

Woolly Bugger

Dressing

Hook: TMC 300, size 6-10.
Thread: Black.
Underbody: Lead wire.
Tail: Black marabou.
Body: Olive chenille.
Rib: Fine gold wire.
Hackle: Dyed black cock.

This big, buggy fly looks like a cross between a streamer and a nymph and mimics a host of prey items from a small fish to a leech or crayfish, and even makes a passable likeness for a big stonefly nymph. It can be tied in various colors, most popular being black, brown, and olive, and can be fished on a floating or sinking line depending on the depth and speed of the water.

GLOSSARY

Collar hackle: A hackle which is wound as a ruff or collar just behind the hook eye.

Cul-de-canard: A soft downy feather found around the preen gland of ducks and geese. Impregnated with natural waterproofing oils, cul-de-canard feathers make ideal wings and hackles for dry flies and emergers.

Dapping: A technique for fishing a fly in windy conditions most often practiced on the large lakes of Scotland and Ireland. It involves using a long rod and a light, floss "blow line" which helps to skip a bushy fly over the water's surface.

Dropper: A short spur of nylon formed by knotting together two lengths of nylon monofilament. One or two can be used to allow extra flies to be fished on the same line.

Dun: The sub-imago of the various species of mayfly, it is the stage which should be copied when the insect is "hatching".

Emerger: Adult aquatic insect breaking free from its nymphal or pupal shuck.

Hackle: Most often a feather from the neck of a chicken used to represent the legs of an insect. For dry flies it is the stiffer cock hackles which are normally used.

Leader: The length of fine nylon monofilament to which the flies are tied. It provides the step from the thick fly line to the fly itself and is used in different lengths and breaking strains depending on the size and type of fly being used.

Lough: The term used for a large lake in Ireland.

Marabou: A soft mobile material used for the wings of lures and tadpoles and the tails of some nymph patterns. Today, marabou comes from the domestic white turkey.

Nymph: This is the immature, aquatic stage of a number of insect groups, notably the mayflies, stoneflies, and dragon and damselflies.

Palmer hackle: A hackle which is wound along the body of a fly rather than just at the eye.

Rib: A material, such as wire or nylon wound as a spiral along the body of a fly. Often used to protect a softer body material, or to add sparkle, it also mimics segmentation in nymph patterns.

Spinner: This is the sexually mature stage of the various species of mayfly. Usually much brighter than the sub-imago.

Tandem: Two or more hooks which are joined together with a flexible link such as strong nylon line. Designed to create a larger fly such as those used to imitate bait fish.

Team: Two or three flies tied to the same leader by using droppers. A method most often used on large lakes.

INDEX

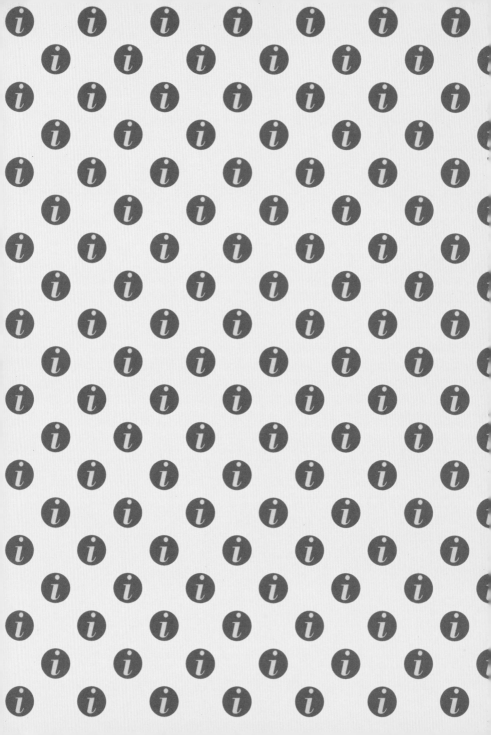